Basic Nail Art Techniques

and how to combine them

Ina of Mynailpolishonline

ISBN:9781973502432

CONTENTS

INTRODUCTION

Having beautiful nails can complement any outfit regardless of the style chosen for the nails or the outfit. The nails can be painted with a subtle or a bold color but adding a little bit of nail art takes the manicure to the next level. Some nail arts can look intimidating from the beginning but the steps for achieving the different styles are often easier than it appears at a first look. Other techniques might take a little time to master but many of the techniques work right away from the start.

The nail art techniques described in this book might require that you know how to use another nail art technique from a previous chapter to be able to complete the nail art, like for example the "Watercolored Flowers" where you should learn the "Watercolor Technique" before trying the Watercolored Flowers.

In every chapter you can find the material needed for the nail art, step by step guides, suggested color combinations and advanced techniques. Under the sub-chapters named "Advanced Techniques" there are some ideas of how to combine the different nail arts with other nail arts presented in the book. In most cases there are examples of how nail arts can be combined with each other and/or examples of color combinations. Many examples have been previously presented as blog posts on the blog "My Nail Polish Online".

BASIC NAIL CARE

Anyone can have beautiful nails, it's just a matter of taking care of them properly. What the nails need varies from one person to another but there are a few guidelines that can usually be applied:

- Keep your nails clean and trim them to a length that suits you. The length of the nails are often dictated by the preferences, the job one has or in some cases by the state of the nails. Strong and non-splitting nails is what everyone wants and that could be a challenge sometimes. Proper caring of the nails can help them get and remain strong and non-splitting.
- Moisturize your hands and nails whenever needed. Hand creme is to be used at least once a day or whenever your hands feel dry. Depending on where you live this is very important especially during winter when the air gets dry.
- Taking care of your cuticles by moisturizing them help the nails remain strong.
- When doing housework as dishes, use gloves to protect your hands and nails from unnecessary contact with water and detergents. Using gloves during housework might also protecting the nails from breakage as you handle the things differently when using gloves.
- Don't bite your nails. Besides the fact that you won't have any nails to talk about after biting them, biting your nails can cause them to grow deformed.
- Always use a base coat when painting your nails. A base coat will prevent your nails from getting too stained from the nail polish and it provides a great base for your manicure.
- Don't use your nails as tools. Using them as tools may cause nail breakages.
- When you happen to break a nail you can always try to repair the damage. There are different methods and repairing kits out there that can keep the damaged nail together until the breakage grows to a level where you can finally cut it or file it.

HOW TO PAINT THE NAILS

The base of a beautiful nail art is always a well applied base color. Therefore painting the base with great care is crucial. Here is how to do it and some general tips.

Choosing the nail polish

The nail polish of your choice should be a fresh one that hasn't been opened for too long. Nail polishes tend to get thicker after a while and the application gets harder with a thick polish. If you still have a polish that you love and that has got thicker by age you could always "save it" by adding a couple of drops of nail polish thinner. Shake the bottle and observe the thickness of the polish. If it isn't flowing well enough repeat the process until you are happy with the result. Don't worry if you have added too much thinner! You could always leave the bottle open for a minute or two and the polish is thicker again. The nail polish thinner is very volatile so you should not wait too long for it to evaporate.

As for choosing the right color, go with your instinct. The colors you feel like wearing are often the ones you should go for. However, some of the colors go better together with others. Therefore there are some suggestions under every chapter with suitable color combinations, but you could always break the rules and try something you think go nice together. In the end, you are the one wearing the manicure, it should express your intuition and color palette.

When it comes to finishes, cremes are often used in nail art. Cremes work great with different tools and they function as great bases. This doesn't mean you should stay away from glitters, holographic polishes or shimmers, but sometimes it's just easier to work with cremes. Whatever finish you are choosing you should try to pick an opaque polish that covers in maximum two coats. Fewer coats make the nail art process much easier.

Step by step

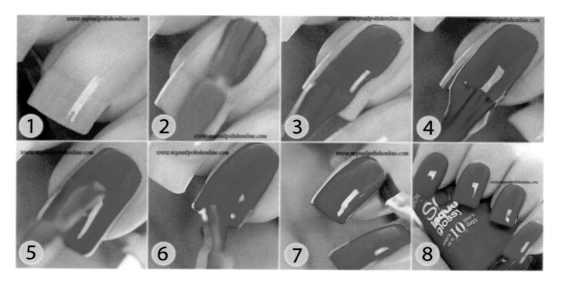

1. Start with a clean nail. The nail should also be free from hand creme, oils or polish residuals. Always start with a base coat. The base coat is important because it protects your nails from getting stained, it prevents chipping and it provides an even base for the polish that you are using. Nails can sometimes have irregularities on the surface. In that case use a base coat that is a ridge-filler. The base coat is usually drying pretty fast so after waiting a minute or two you can continue painting your nails with the desired base color.
2. Start painting your nails from the cuticles. Make sure you place the nail polish brush close to the cuticle without being so close that polish is flowing into the cuticles. The nail polish brush shouldn't have too much polish on it or the polish will end up flooding your cuticles.
3. Move the brush from the cuticle to the nail tip.
4. Repeat the movement on the right side of the nail.
5. Repeat the movement on the left of the nail.
6. Go over the nail tip line with the nail polish brush. This will prolong your manicure. If necessary, apply a second coat of polish the same way as the first coat. While many polishes cover in one coat you should consider applying a second coat to give the manicure more durability and a deeper base color.
7. Clean up the cuticles. This is done with a small nail art brush and some nail polish remover or acetone. Acetone gets you faster results but it's more damaging for your skin, nails and hands. The brush used for the clean up should be small and wide. Some people prefer using an angled nail art brush for the clean up but it works with any small and wide nail art brush.
8. Finish by applying a fast drying top coat.

Painting the dominant hand

Let's face it, it's easier to paint with your dominant hand than to paint THE dominant hand. That shouldn't stop you from trying though. Practice makes perfect and while the first tries might seem a little insecure, with time you could come to the point where you are painting most of the techniques equally well on both hands. Some tips for an easier application and easier painting of your dominant hand are:

- Start by painting your dominant hand. You have most patience in the beginning of the nail art which improves the chance is that you'll get best results if you start by painting your dominant hand.
- Keep your dominant hand steady placed on your working space and if possible rotate, tilt or move the dominant hand while you are painting it.
- Keep the non-dominant hand steady while painting.

Freehanding contra Guides

Some of the looks can be achieved in two ways, by freehanding or by using guides. Each technique has it's advantages and disadvantages so choose the technique that suits you. The manicures done with guides look often more impeccable than those done by freehanding but there is a catch! You have to have patience for a manicure done with guides to look great. The base of your manicure must dry completely before you continue with the guides otherwise you will end up lifting off the base coat when you remove your guides. Experiment with both techniques and you will soon find your favorite.

NAIL ART TOOLS

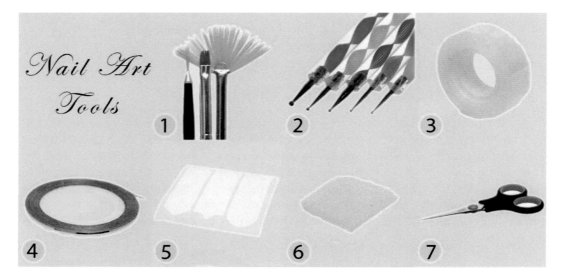

To paint some of the nail art techniques described in the following chapters you won't need any additional tools beside nail polishes, like the freehanded "French tips", but most of the techniques require some kind of tools. Here are the most frequently used tools:

1. Nail art brushes. The most frequently used nail art brush is a thin one with a small end. If your thinnest nail art brush doesn't produce lines that are thin enough, consider trimming it to the point where you are happy with the result. Always cut the bristles of the nail art brush close to the handle of the brush. The flat nail art brush (it could be angled or not) is used for cleaning up the cuticles. The fan brush is used for the "Fan Brush Technique".
2. Dotting tools. These can be replaced by bobby pins, toothpicks, pens or anything with a sharper end like a pen. The dotting tools are mostly used for "Dotticures" but they can also be used for "Needle marbling", "Needle marbled flowers" or for "Galaxy Nails".
3. Tape is good to have in some techniques. The tape is primary used to protect your cuticles from polish that fasten on unwanted places like cuticles as in "Water Marbling" and "Water Spotted Manicures" but it can also be used as guides in some techniques.
4. Nail art tape. This tape is very thin and is mostly used for "Stripes".
5. Guides. The guides are used for some techniques like "Chevrons", "French Tips" or "Ruffian".

6. A piece of a sponge is sometimes needed for some techniques like for example the "Gradients". Try cutting a piece of a kitchen sponge or a makeup sponge. You should cut the sponge small enough to have control of the result on the nails.

7. A pair of scissors comes in handy for cutting decals or newspapers for "Water Decals" or "Newspaper Nails".

ACCENT NAILS

An accent nail is a nail that differs from the other nails when it comes to color or pattern. All the techniques can be used as accent nails so it's up to you to decide if you want all the nails to look the same or if you want to add an accent. You could also use accent nails when the nail art techniques are crowded or time consuming. In the left picture above the accent nail has a flower as an accent nail while the right picture above has a different colored nail as an accent that also has a leopard spot pattern painted on it.

There are many variations on accent nails from having one nail that is different from the other to having all nails different as in the pictures above. The latter design is called "Skittle".

ANIMAL PRINT

The notion "Animal Print" is wide but in nail art there are a couple of patterns that are usually painted, the leopard spots and the zebra stripes.

Leopard Spots

www.mynailpolishonline.com

Leopard spots are easy to do and oh so eye-catching! That's why these kinds of designs are often painted and I too am often wearing them in different colors, as accents or as full manicures, during spring, summer, autumn and winter. They are timeless!

Materials/Supplies

This is what you need for painting leopard spots:
- A polish for your base, preferably a light color
- Two polishes for the spots. Choose a darker polish for the outside of the spots

and a lighter polish for the inside of the spots.
- A dotting tool or a toothpick
- Top coat

Step by step

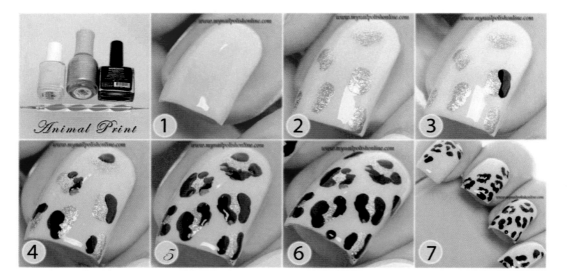

1. Apply your base polish and let it dry. Use a fast drying top coat to speed up the drying process.
2. With the lighter polish and the dotting tool paint some random spots on the nails.
3. Clean the dotting tool and paint some darker spots around the lighter spots with the darker polish. They should not be too symmetrical, try to do some random work here too.
4. Continue adding random shaped spots around the lighter spots.
5. Paint spots until the lighter spots are surrounded almost on every side. Leave some room though for the light polish to show it's edges.
6. You can also add dots between the spots. These dots are optional and they don't have to surround a lighter color.
7. Finish with a top coat.

Zebra stripes

By wearing zebra prints on your nails with the traditional color combination like a white base and black lines you will assure that your nails will get noticed. You can paint the zebra stripes oblique as in the step by step sub chapter below or parallel to your nail tips, or any other directions you like.

Materials/Supplies

The materials needed for the Zebra Stripes are:
- A polish for your background
- A polish for the stripes
- A thin nail art brush
- Top coat

Step by step

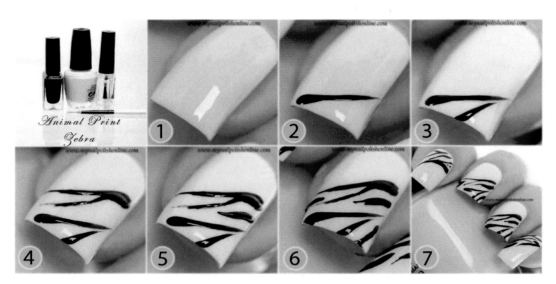

1. Start by applying your base color.
2. Take the nail art brush dipped into the second color and paint an oblique line on your nail. The line should be thicker at one end and thinner at the other end. Don't worry about painting the line uneven, the real zebra stripes aren't perfect or even either.
3. Place a second line/stripe on the nail forming an angle between the two lines. Make the line thicker at the same end as the first one.
4. Paint more lines joined in an angle with a thicker end and a thinner end.
5. Place another line, between the two groups of lines.
6. Add lines until you are happy with the design.
7. Clean up and add a top coat.

Suggested color combination

The classic color combination for leopard spots is using a nude polish as a base, brown for the inner parts of the spots and black (or darker brown) for the outer part of the spots. You could also try the snow leopard using white as a base, light gray for the inner part of the spots and darker gray for the outer part of the spots. As long as your inside of the spots is lighter as the outside, you could combine almost any colors, like white base and purple/black spots, green base and brown/black spots, gold base and red/black spots as shown above etc.

For the Zebra print the classic color combination is white as a background and black for the stripes. Other colors that also look great together are black and gold as in the picture above, aqua and black as in the right picture below, pink and black or any contrasting colors you would like to have.

Advanced techniques

The leopard print can be used on top of many of the previous techniques, like on top of gradients, saran wraps, watercolored backgrounds. You could also paint the leopard spots only on one part of the nail leaving room for other nail art designs like zebra stripes. On the left picture below the animal print is painted over a Saran wrap while on the right picture below you can see a mixtures of colors and a blend with zebra stripes.

NEWSPAPER PRINT

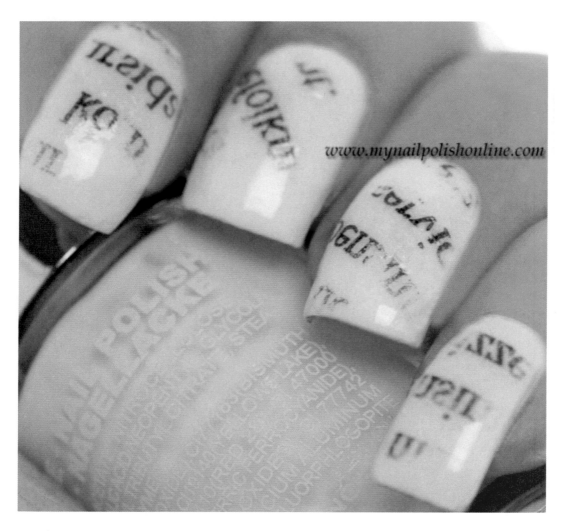

The newspaper print can stand for themselves but look also amazing as backgrounds to other nail arts. Combining them with dusty, pale shades you could create great vintage nails. They are usually a little bit tricky because the end result depends on the quality of the newspaper used for this technique.

Materials/Supplies

This is what is needed for the newspaper print:
- A light colored polish for your base
- A newspaper that is new (not a couple of days old). New prints detaches easier from the paper than older ones.
- Makeup tissues
- Matte top coat (this is optional)
- Alcohol or water
- Top coat

Step by step

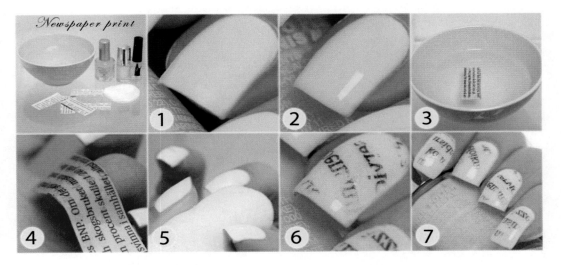

1. Apply your base coat and let it dry. It is important that the base of your manicure is completely dry before you start with the newspapers. Use a fast drying top coat to speed up the drying process.
2. Add a matte top coat to make the newspaper print adhere easier. This step is optional.
3. When the base is completely dry, cut a bit of newspaper with the chosen print and dip it into the alcohol or water. The print won't be able to be read on your nails because the script will be mirrored so what it actually says on the paper isn't important.
4. Make sure most of the water is gone from the paper and press the newspaper bit onto your nail with the print facing down.
5. Press with a makeup tissue over the newspaper. This will remove the extra water or alcohol and it will also help the print to transfer easier.
6. Wait for a short period of time (about a half minute or more) and slowly lift up the newspaper from your nail. Some of the print will be left on the nails if everything went right.
7. Top coat the manicure.

Troubleshooting

The first thing you need to try if the print hasn't transferred to the nails is to apply a coat of matte top coat if you haven't done that yet. If the print still hasn't transferred to the nails try with another fresh newspaper. It is important that the newspaper is wet when you press it onto the nails but not soaked with water. If too much water stays on the newspaper it can prevent the script from translating to the nails. If it's still not working, try going from water to alcohol or from alcohol to water. Alcohol evaporates faster and is usually used for newspaper nails but the technique also works with plain water.

Suggested color combinations

Because newspaper print is usually black the base color should be chosen to be a light one. A white or an off-white are usually used but you could also try a minty polish or a nude polish for a vintage look.

Advanced techniques

The newspaper technique works as a great background for roses as in the right picture above or other flowers that you would want to paint. It could also be combined with water decals. Try darkening the edges using the watercolor technique and a darker polish as in the left picture above.

DRY BRUSH TECHNIQUE

This could be one of the most colorful and eye catching nail art if you use contrasting colors (maybe neons), a light colored base and a black polish. The nail art is easy and fast to do and you won't even need any other materials or supplies besides nail polish.

Materials/Supplies

These are the materials needed for the Dry Brush Technique:
- A white or a light colored polish for the base
- A couple of different polishes for the brush strokes
- Top coat

Step by step

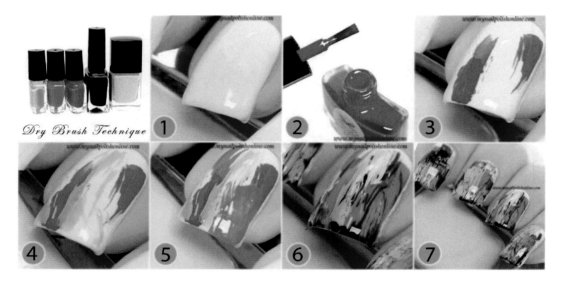

1. Start by painting your nails with the light colored polish. Light colored polishes have often difficult formulas and require several coats to cover. You won't need the base to be perfect so if the base hasn't covered completely it's OK. Let the base polish dry and add a top coat to speed up the drying process.
2. Take one of the colors and wipe the excess polish from the brush onto the neck of the bottle. You need to have the brush almost dry from polish.
3. With the wiped brush, paint some random strokes on the nails. Start from different places on different nails and leave room for the next color/colors and for the black polish.
4. Repeat the process in step two and three with the second color.
5. Repeat once again the process in step two and three with the next color.
6. Finish by adding black strokes here and there. Make sure some light spots coming from the base color are still visible.
7. Clean up and seal the result with a top coat.

Suggested color combinations

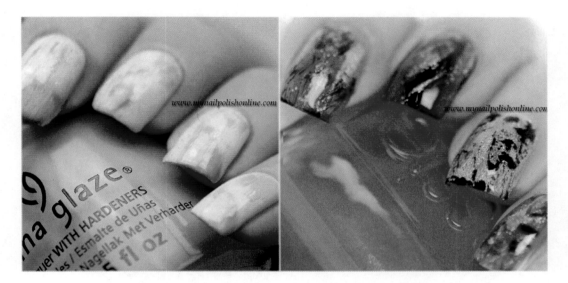

The technique above works very nicely with a white base and some contrasting colors like pink, yellow, green and red.The dry brush technique also works beautifully with a dark base (e.g. a black) and some metallic polishes like metallic green, gold and red. Experiment with different color combinations and find your favorites that way.

Advanced techniques

The dry brush technique itself is crowded and if you want to combine it with other techniques I would suggest doing a pale color combination that leaves space for freehanding with a contrasting polish like black.

You could also combine this technique with french tips or half moons, or maybe adding a colored frame around the nail with a thin nail art brush as in the picture above.

FRENCH TIPS

It's really hard to find a manicure that is more elegant and classic than French Tips or a French Manicure. The classic French Manicure has a clear, a sheer nude or a pale sheer pink as a base and a white tip. The manicure emulates the look of a well taken care, natural nail with the white nail tip and the natural nail base. There are two ways of painting French Tips, by using guides of by freehanding. There are pros and cons with both methods so let's take a look at them.

Using Guides

If you want to have perfect lines for your French tips then you'll have to use guides. The only catch is that you'll have to wait for the base polish to be completely dry before you start using the guides. The flawless result is well worth the wait though.

Materials/Supplies

The following materials are needed for doing French Tips using guides:
- A polish for your base
- A contrasting polish for the nail tips
- Guides or tape
- Top coat

Step by step

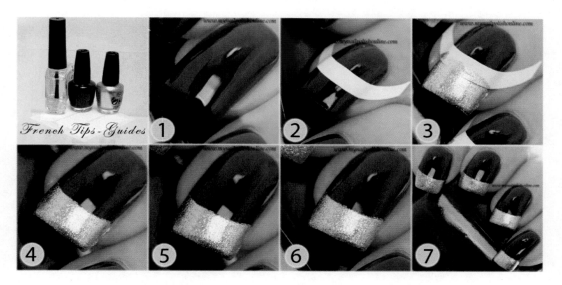

1. Apply the base polish and let it dry. When using guides the base polish must be completely dry before proceeding to the next step. A fast drying top coat will speed up the process.
2. Fasten the guides at the tip of the nails leaving room for the contrasting polish.
3. Paint the tips with the contrasting polish.
4. Wait for a minute or two for the polish to dry enough. Remove the guides carefully.
5. Cleanup the cuticles.
6. If the contrasting polish has bled under the guides you could try to remove carefully some of the excess color with a nail art brush and nail polish remover or acetone. Thanks to the top coat applied in step 1 you will be able to do that but be careful to not overdo it or you will end up with bald spots. You could also correct the line by covering the imperfections with a small nail art brush dipped into the base color. The top coat will heal the visible patch afterward.
7. Top coat the manicure.

Freehanding

Freehanding nail tips is the easiest way of doing French tips because you don't have to have a completely dry base to paint the tips. However you have to be steady on your hands, but that comes with a little bit of practice.

Materials/Supplies

Freehanding French Tips requires only the following materials:
- A polish for your base
- A contrasting polish for the nail tips
- Top coat

Step by step

1. Start by applying the base polish and let it dry.
2. Wait for a couple of minutes and then start painting the tips on the nails with a contrasting nail polish. To paint straight lines you might have to practice a couple of times before you'll get the types of lines you want. However there is one thing you could try in order to be able to paint the tip lines the way you want them to be. When painting the tip lines, rotate the nail you are painting on instead of the brush. That will give you more control during the painting.
3. If you need or want to adjust the lines you can reinforce them with a second line going over the first one. You need to paint this one a little bit thicker though in order to cover the first one. Keeping the brush flat over the nail as in the picture above will also give you more control over the tip line.
4. Clean up around the cuticles.
5. Apply a top coat.

Suggested color combinations

While the classic look is nude/sheer polish as a base and white tips as in the right picture above where the manicure is also topped with a flake polish, there are a lot of variations that can be done with this technique. The colored variations of this manicure are called Funky French and they can be almost any two colors together.

Some of the color combinations that look great together are:

- Black base and gold or silver tips
- Gray base and minty tips
- Nude base and orange or neon tips
- Glittery tips are also a variation of funky french. For example try using a white base and blue glittery tips as in the picture below.

Advanced techniques

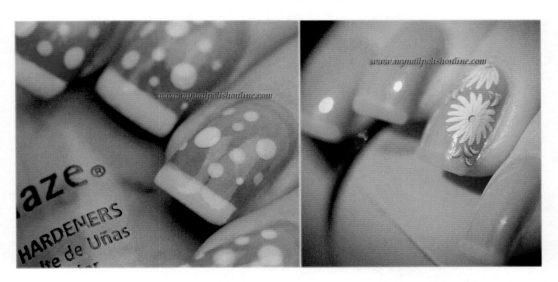

Both French Manicures or Funky French can be great bases for different manicures. Use them together with flowers, dots, glitter top coats or water decals as in the two pictures above.

DOTTICURES

Dot manicures, often called dotticures or polka dots are one of the easiest way of nail art that is so much fun! The possibilities of combining dots are endless and you'll only have to have fun with this nail art technique to succeed.

Materials/Supplies

This is what you need for dotticures:
- Nail polish for the base
- One or two polishes for the dots
- One or two dotting tools, toothpicks, bobby pins or something with similar ends
- A piece of paper
- Top coat

Step by step

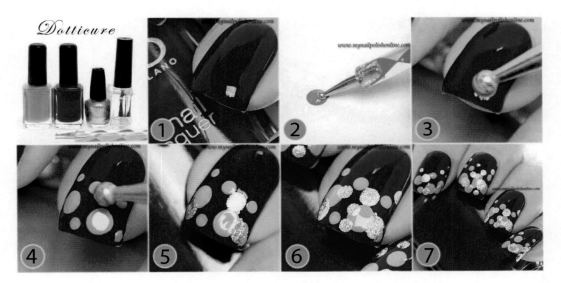

1. Start by painting your nails with the base color of your choice.
2. Put some nail polish on the piece of paper and dip the dotting tool into the nail polish.
3. Start placing dots on the nails.
4. If you are applying them as a gradient, place most of them at the nail tips. If you are using more than one size of the dotting tools, switch to the other size and apply also these dots on the nails.
5. If you are applying more than one color, switch to the second color and place the dots on the nails the same way as you did with the first color. Repeat the process with all the colors you are using for the dotticure.
6. Clean up around the cuticles if necessary.
7. Apply the top coat.

Suggested color combinations

Any colors will go here so pick your favorites and start dotting. Black and whites will go with any color so if you hesitate, try combining your favorite color with black or white dots or just combine black and white. Use different finishes as creme bases and shimmer dots or the other way around.

Advanced techniques

Dots work perfectly with flowers. Paint flowers as accent nails or use water decals together with dots, as in the left picture above.

For a more interesting look, try dotting smaller dots inside of the bigger dots. This will give the illusion of painted rings instead of a dot in dot. An example is the black and white dotticure shown left above.

Dots can be spread evenly on the nails, bigger and smaller dots can be combined in patterns and you can paint dots in a gradient. Everything works when it comes to dots.

WATERCOLOR TECHNIQUE

This technique works nicely on it's own but it also works as a great background for different kind of nail arts. The watercolor technique is inspired by the artistic watercolor paintings and even if no water is involved in this technique the result looks like the paintings done with watercolors. When using watercolors the solvent is water but when we use polishes we have to use acetone or polish remover instead to obtain the same result as in the watercolor arts.

Materials/Supplies

Following materials are needed for this technique:
- A polish for your base, preferably a light color
- One or several polishes for the watercolor technique
- Polish remover or acetone
- A nail art brush
- A piece of paper
- Top coat

Step by step

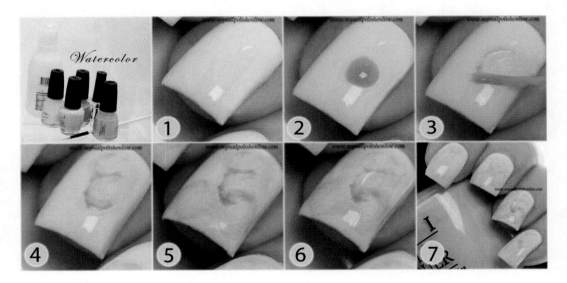

1. Start by applying the base of your manicure and top coat the manicure. This is important since we are going to work with acetone or polish remover on top of the base coat. The top coat is acting like a shield between the base polish and the acetone/polish remover used for in technique. The design is easier to obtain and see if the base color is light.
2. Place a little bit of nail polish on the nail and dip your nail art brush into the acetone.
3. Start diluting the nail polish with the acetone (or nail polish remover) on your nail. If you think it's too much nail polish remove a part of it with the nail art brush. If too much acetone comes on your nails you can remove the excess with the same nail art brush.
4. Create different patterns on the nails by repeating the process in step two and three.
5. If you are using more than one color switch to the next color and repeat the process in step two, three and four.
6. If you are using a third color do the same thing with it.
7. Top coat the manicure when you're happy with the result.

Suggested color combinations

A light base is often easier to work with than a dark base even if a dark base also can give beautiful results. Try something similar to:

- A white base and any colored polish for the watercolors as in the right picture above where black is used for the watercolor patterns
- A pink base and purple polish for the watercolor
- A blue base and green polish for the watercolor
- A black base can sometimes be used as a background. The polishes used together with a black background must be opaque to be able to contrast a little bit with the black color. Try using white or red as in the left picture above.

Advanced techniques

The watercolor technique can be used with great success as a base for other designs like flowers, feathers or any other designs you can think of. It can also be used for darkening edges to create a vintage look. Using a dark base for a lighter watercolor design is often challenging but the result could be stunning.

Experiment with different color combinations and choose your favorite combination for your design. For a delicate look use the watercolor technique for the flower petals as in the two pictures above where the bases of the flowers have been done with the watercolor technique. The watercolored flowers are described in more detail in the chapter Watercolored Flowers.

FRAMED NAILS

There is something special about framed nails and with the right colors it could look pretty amazing. Framed nails can be used on their own and in combination with other nail art techniques. The technique involves freehanding and it requires a steady hand.

Materials/Supplies

The following materials are needed for Framed Nails:
- A polish for your base
- A polish for the frame
- A thin nail art brush
- Top coat

Step by step

1. Apply the base polish and let it dry. A fast drying top coat will speed up the process.
2. Start by painting thin lines (frames) around the nails with a thin nail art brush. Begin at the cuticles.
3. Continue on one side of the nail.
4. Now paint the other side.
5. Finish by painting the nail tip.
6. Clean up around the cuticles.
7. Top coat the manicure.

Suggested color combinations

For a dramatic look try using contrasting colors like white and black, red and black, red or black and gold or yellow and black as in the picture above. If you want a subtle look use pastel colors or colors that are similar. If your frames don't turn up perfect the subtle look is a good way to go because the imperfections will be camouflaged by your color choice.

Advanced techniques

You could frame almost any nail art you are painting, for example flowers, fan brush techniques as in the left picture above, saran wraps, splatters, watercolor manicures, dry brush techniques as in the right picture above etc. Experiment with the unexpected and you might be amazed by the result.

GRADIENTS

Gradients can be so eye-catchy! There are several types of gradients but all of them are done according to the same principle, one polish goes into another creating a zone where the two colors are blended in some way. All polish types are suitable for gradients but there are two techniques for applying the gradients: The Sponging technique and the Glitter Technique.

The sponging technique

This technique is used for doing gradients between two polishes with the same finish as two cremes, two glitters etc. but also for blending cremes with shimmers, cremes with holos and shimmers with holos.

Materials/Supplies

This is what is needed for sponging gradients:
- Two polishes for the gradient
- A little sponge
- A piece of paper
- Orange stick, toothpick or dotting tool
- A pair of tweezer (this is optional)
- Top coat

Step by step

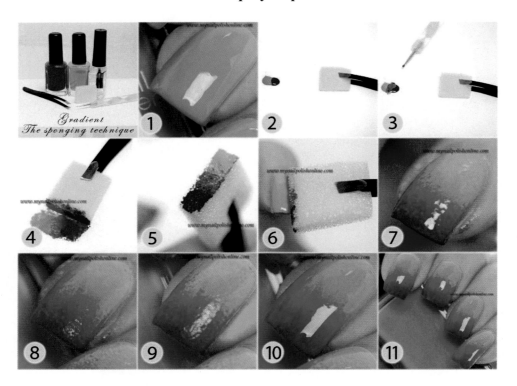

1. Decide the direction of the gradient. Which color is going to be at the tip of the nails and which is going to be at your cuticles? Paint your nails with the polish that you're going to use at your cuticles. The polish doesn't need to cover perfectly, but it should cover most of the surface of the nails.
2. Place the two polishes that are going to be used for the gradient next to each other on the paper.
3. Take the orange stick, a toothpick or a dotting tool and blend a small region of the two polishes that are lying next to each other.
4. Pick up the polishes with the sponge.
5. The sponge should have one polish on one end, the other polish at the other end and a region where the two polishes are blended.
6. Start sponging the nails.

7. Be sure to be sponging a little bit up and down the nails to create a smoother gradient.
8. Repeat until you're happy with the result.
9. Clean up around the cuticles with a nail art brush and the nail polish remover.
10. Apply the top coat. Here is where the magic really happens. The top coat makes the gradient even smoother and more beautiful than it was before. Don't wait for the gradient to dry completely before you're applying the top coat if you want to create a smooth gradient.
11. The gradient is finished now. Keep it this way or use it as a base for other nail arts.

The glitter technique

This technique is much less messy than the sponge technique. The effect this technique creates is spectacular though.

Materials/Supplies

The materials for this technique are:
- A creme polish for your base
- A glitter for the gradient
- Top coat

Step by Step

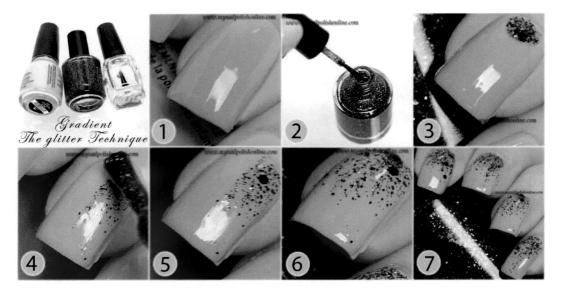

1. Start by applying the base color of your choice and let it dry. Speed up the drying process by applying a fast drying top coat.
2. Take the glitter polish brush and wipe most of the glitters from the brush.
3. Place a small portion of glitter on the nail next to the cuticle or at the nail tip.
4. Drag strokes with the glitter brush creating a gradient on the nail, beginning at the cuticles or at the nail tips.
5. While you are dragging the glitter with the brush, most of the glitter should stay at the cuticles or nail tips.
6. The glitter should end before the nail ends. A portion of creme polish should remain without glitter.
7. Apply a top coat.

Suggested color combinations

For gradients, try combining colors close to each other or contrasting colors. This is valid both for glitter gradients and for creme and shimmer gradients. Some of the color combinations that would look great together are:

- A light pink and a dark pink work nicely as in the middle left picture above
- Black and a contrasting color
- White and a contrasting color as yellow, purple or blue as in the upper right picture above
- Turquoise, teal or aqua and gold

Advanced techniques

One of the advanced techniques is using more than two colors for creating a gradient as in the middle right picture in the sub-chapter "Suggested color combinations" above. You could also complete the gradient with flowers as in the left picture above, dots or french tips as in the right picture above.

RUFFIANS

The easiest way to paint ruffians is by freehanding them. The design looks and is build up as two nail polish layers on top of each other leaving a small margin for the polish underneath to be visible. The technique requires a steady hand but it isn't more difficult than painting your nails as usual, only you do it twice.

Freehanded Ruffians

If you are painting your nails frequently then you will be able to freehand ruffians without a problem. The freehanded ruffians might have a little bit of imperfections but they can be corrected before you apply the topcoat. You could also hide the imperfections with an extra line painted between the two colors that build the ruffian.

Materials/Supplies

You only need a couple of polishes for ruffians:
- A polish for your background
- An opaque polish for the upper layer of the ruffian
- Top coat

Step by step

1. Apply the polish chosen as your base and apply a fast drying top coat on top of it. The fast drying top coat serves two things: it helps the base polish do dry faster and it allows you to correct and clean up the second layer of polish before you apply the finishing top coat.
2. Start applying the second layer of polish that has a contrasting color to the base starting in the middle of the nail a bit down from your cuticle. When you choose this polish you should make sure it is opaque in one coat to assure you cover the first one at once.
3. Continue painting the nail as if you were going to paint a smaller nail on top of the applied nail polish.
4. If the lines aren't as straight as you would like them to be you could take a small angled nail art brush that has been dipped into nail polish remover (or acetone) and correct the lines. You have to work fast now and don't work too much on the same spot or the protecting layer of top coat will dissolve and you could end up removing the base polish too.
5. Apply the top coat.

Ruffian by Guides

In this technique you will need one more additional thing compared to the freehanding technique: rounded guides.

Materials/Supplies

The complete list of materials is as follows:
- A polish for your background
- An opaque polish for the upper layer of the ruffian
- Rounded nail guides
- Top coat

Step by step

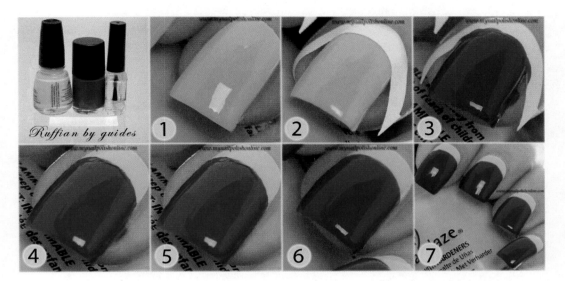

1. Apply the polish chosen as your base and apply a fast drying top coat on top of it.
2. Apply the nail guides at the cuticles. The base polish must be completely dry before the nail guides are applied, otherwise they will lift up parts of the base polish upon removal.
3. Apply the second polish on the part of the nails that is free from nail guides.
4. Remove the nail guides.
5. Clean up around the cuticles with a thin nail art brush and some nail polish remover.
6. If the lines aren't as straight as you would like them to be you could take a small angled nail art brush that has been dipped into nail polish remover (or acetone) and correct the lines. You have to work fast here and don't work too much on the same spot or the protecting layer of top coat will dissolve and you could end up removing the base polish too.
7. Apply the top coat.

Suggested color combinations

Metallics together with cremes work perfectly together, but so do the same kinds of finishes like cremes with cremes, and metallics with metallics. Glitters are harder to incorporate in ruffians but they can make a great base for a ruffian depending on the sizes of the glitters. Here are some suggestions you could try:

- Black base and white/red/gold as the upper layer
- Off-white and gray/green
- Orange, purple and gold as in the left picture below
- Different shades and finishes of the same color as a metallic/shimmer green base and a creme on top of that
- You might want to stay away from red backgrounds as they can make your cuticles look bloody. However that could be a great effect for a Halloween manicure.

Advanced techniques

A variation of the ruffian technique is to do an extra line along the line that divides the background polish from the polish that you have applied on top of it as in the two pictures above. If you have a steady hand, this extra line can cover for some of the imperfections that may occur when applying the upper polish. You could also do several layers of ruffians on top of each other.

FAN BRUSH TECHNIQUE

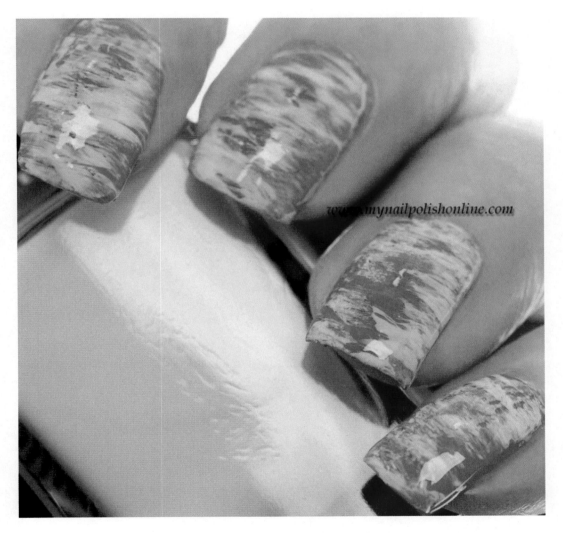

The fine lines created by the fan brush technique are hard to obtain with other techniques. The technique is usually used for doing horizontal brush strokes but it could also be used in other directions.

Materials/Supplies

For the Fan Brush Technique you will need:
- A polish for your background
- A fan brush
- A polish or two for your fan brush strokes
- Top coat

Step by step

1. Start by applying the base polish.
2. Dip the fan brush into one of the additional colors that you want to use for the fan brush strokes. Make sure the fan brush isn't drenched into the polish.
3. Start applying brush strokes to the nails.
4. Repeat applying brush strokes from one side of the nail to another.
5. If you use several polishes, change to the next one and continue applying brush strokes from one side to another.
6. Clean up the cuticles with a nail art brush and nail polish remover or acetone.
7. Top coat the manicure.

Suggested color combinations

The technique can be used with almost any color combinations. Here are some suggestions:

- Whites can be combined with any other color you like, like blue or pink or yellow
- Blues combine perfectly with other shades of blue or with purples/magentas
- Pinks work great with white, magenta, purple, black, gray
- Greens work great with yellows and browns
- You can also match colors that are close to each other like magenta and orange with aqua as in the picture above.

Advanced techniques

Use more than one color for the brush strokes. You could blend the colors or do several blocks with colors. A gradient done with brush strokes and the fan brush would work too.

The fan brush technique can be used on it's own or as accent nails for different manicures or combinations. It can also be combined with funky french tips as in the left part of the picture above, frames, flowers or both frames and flowers as in the right part of the picture above.

WATER DECALS

    This is one of the easiest type of nail art because the art is already painted by others and you will only need to place it on the nails. However there are a couple of things one needs to think about while using water decals but when you master them you will be able to do amazing nail art without any effort.

Materials/Supplies

The materials needed for water decals are:
- A polish for your background
- Water decals
- Scissors
- A pair of tweezers
- Water
- Makeup tissues
- Top coat

Step by step

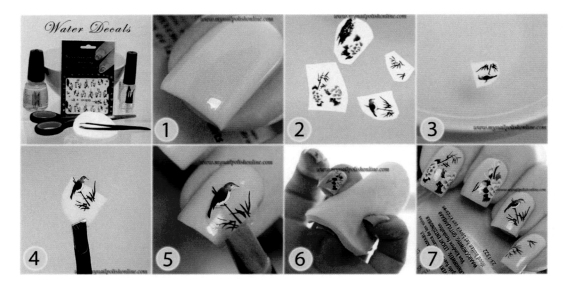

1. Start by applying the base polish of your manicure. Your base must be completely dry before you start working with water decals. Apply a fast drying top coat if you want the base polish to dry faster.
2. Remove the water decals from the plastic bag and remove the top plastic layer that lays in top of them. Cut around the water decals with a pair of scissors. Some water decals only have a small area of plastic around them whilst others are done on a big sheet of plastic. You'll have to be more precise on your cutting when you're cutting the ones you want from the latter one.
3. Place the cut decals in water for about 10-15 seconds or until the pattern releases from the background paper.
4. Try to see if they are ready to use by detaching the background paper from the decal.
5. When the decals are easy to detach from the paper that they are placed on, place the decals onto your nails with the side that faced the paper now facing the nails. Use a pair of tweezers to handle the decals. You could add a little bit of water to

the nails to be able to move the decals back and forth on the nails until you have found the right position for them.

6. When the decals are on place on the nails remove the extra water with the makeup tissue.

7. Top coat the manicure.

Suggested color combinations

You'll have to choose the background of your manicure in accordance to the decals. In general, light backgrounds are easier to use together with decals unless the decals are the same color as the background.

Advanced techniques

Use water decals together with sponged backgrounds, gradients or saran wraps for a more sophisticated look as in the right picture above where the decals together with the sponged background have created a vintage look.

You can also use water decals as accent nails together with other nail art techniques like dotticures and French Tips as in the left picture above.

You'll have to choose the background of your manicure in accordance to the decals. In general, light backgrounds are easier to use together with decals unless the decals are the same color as the background.

FLORAL MANICURES

Floral manicures are perfect to wear during the summertime but they can also cheer up a winter day when the snow is falling outside and the days are shorter and darker. There are many types of floral manicures but some of the most used are "Five Petal Flowers", "Roses", "Flowers using needle marbling" and "Watercolored flowers".

Five petal flowers

One kind of flowers that are really easy to paint and that look great on the nails are the basic five petal flowers. The design is easy and effective. The effect created could be light, striking or dramatic depending on the colors of the painted flowers.

Materials/Supplies

The following materials are needed for painting five petal flowers:

- A polish for your base
- One (or several) polishes for the flowers
- A black polish for the anthers
- A thin nail art brush
- Top coat

Step by step

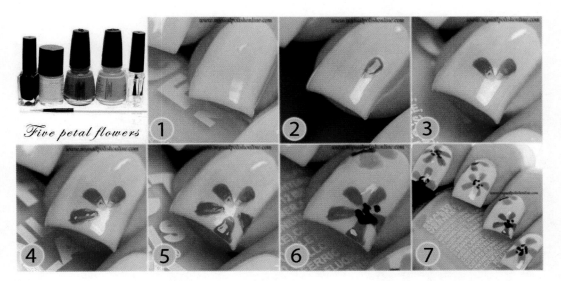

1. Apply your base polish and let it dry.
2. With the thin nail art brush start painting the first petal using the polish chosen for the flower petals.
3. Place the second petal next to the first one leaving a little bit of space between them.
4. Continue with the next petal.
5. Paint the rest of the petals.
6. You can either stop here or continue painting some dots in the middle of the flowers. Paint the other flowers the same way.
7. Top coat the manicure.

Suggested color combinations

Many colors work together when it comes to these kind of flowers. Here are some color suggestions:

- Green bases with white flowers
- Nude bases with pink/red/purple/navy blue flowers as in the left picture above
- Clear bases with any kind of colors for the flowers as in the right picture above
- Pink bases with white/red/purple/navy blue flowers

Advanced techniques

One of my favorite way to combine these kinds of flowers is to go over the petals with a second color. Don't paint the entire petal, just the inside of it. For the insides of the petals you could use a different shade of the same color used for the petals, like a darker pink or a lighter pink as in the left part of the picture above. Combine these flowers with funky french tips, saran wraps, watercolor techniques, gradients or framed nails as in the right part of the picture above where the base is done with the watercolor technique.

Roses

There's something magical with a rose manicure! The end result can look spring-ish or vintage depending on the color combinations and the mixture of the techniques. They seem a little bit complicated to do but the steps involved are much easier than one might think.

Materials/Supplies

The following materials are needed for painting the roses:
- A polish for your base
- Two shades of pink for the flowers
- A green polish for the leafs
- A dotting tool or a bobby pin
- A thin nail art brush
- Top coat

Step by step

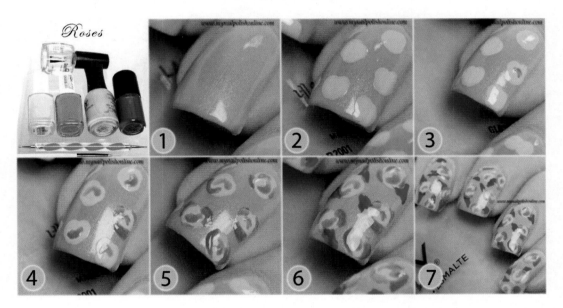

1. Start by applying a base and let it dry. Apply a fast drying top coat to speed up the process.
2. Paint some bigger spots with the light pink polish and the dotting tool.
3. With the thin nail art brush and the darker pink, start painting some "C"shapes into the light pink spots.
4. Continue with more "C"-shapes within the light pink areas. Some of them should be on the outer part of the light pink areas.
5. Finish by adding even more "C"-shapes.
6. Paint leafs with the green polish.
7. Apply a top coat.

Suggested color combinations

A light background such as light pink, white, light blue or even light green builds a great base for roses but even darker shades are great looking backgrounds. It all depends on the feeling you want to give to the manicure. The light background is perfect for spring and summer while the darker backgrounds as in the right part of the picture above work well in autumn and winter.

For the roses, try two shades of the same color, like a light and a darker pink, a light and a darker purple or a light and a darker yellow. Try also white with lighter shades and pink with red. Blue and purple shades and pink and purple shades work great together too.

Advanced techniques

The roses can be combined with a gradient as a background as in the left part of the picture above, with dots or with stripes. They can be painted randomly on the nails or just one bigger rose at the cuticles. The roses can also be used as an accent on one or two nails.

Flowers using needle marbling

This is one of the easiest way of doing flowers. The flowers done by using this technique are not only easy to do but also stylish. You want to practice on a piece of paper first though just to get the technique right. The flowers can be placed randomly on the nails or in a pattern like a Funky French manicure.

Materials/Supplies

The materials needed for these flowers are:
- Nail polish for the base
- One or two polishes for the flowers. The polishes chosen for the flowers should be opaque cremes
- A polish in a contrasting polish for the anther of the flowers
- A dotting tool or a toothpick
- A small dotting tool or a needle
- Top coat

Step by step

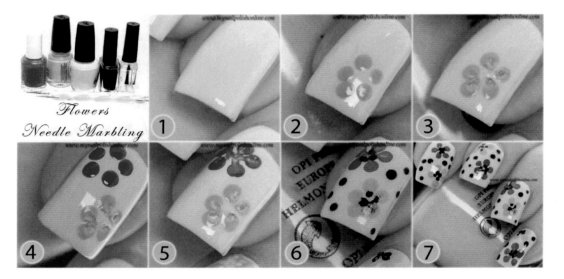

1. Apply your base polish and let it dry. Apply a fast drying top coat if necessary.
2. With a dotting tool place some dots (five would be a great number) in a circle on the nails leaving some space in the middle of them.
3. Take a dotting tool or a needle and drag a line from the middle of the dots to the middle of the circle created by the dots.
4. Place five more dots with the same color or with a second color on a different place on the nail.
5. Repeat step three for the new dot set. Paint as many flowers you wish to on every nail.
6. When you've finished creating the petals of the flowers place some dots in the middle part of the flowers with a contrasting color like black if you are using light colors for the background. Use a dotting tool for that. You could also place some random dots with the contrasting color on the nails. This part is optional.
7. Apply a fast drying top coat.

Suggested color combinations

White or pale backgrounds work beautifully with pink, purple or orange flowers. For the anthers of the flowers, paint those dots in a contrasting color such as black, white or yellow. You can also use dark backgrounds with light colored flowers. You could also try combining a dark background with medium colored flowers like medium red and purple as in the picture above.

Advanced techniques

Needle flowers can be painted on gradient backgrounds as a change.

Flowers using the Watercolor Technique

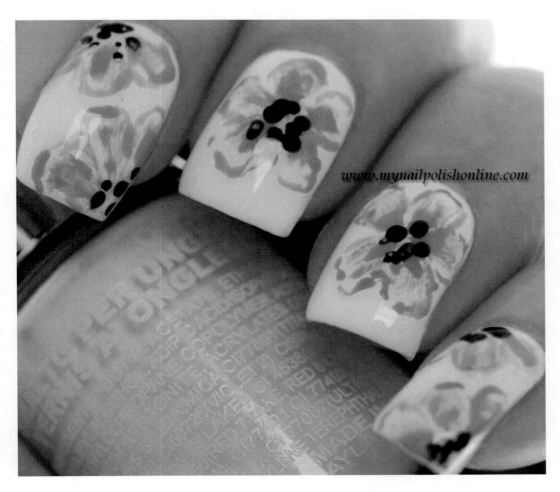

www.mynailpolishonline.com

Flowers can be done in so many ways! The watercolor technique adds a little bit of a dreamy, poetic look to the flowers. The washed out effect produced by the watercolor technique can be combined with contrasting lines. Contrast is often wanted in nail art even if there are manicures that look great as subtle manicures.

Materials/Supplies

The materials needed for the watercolored flowers are:
- A light colored polish for the base
- A contrasting polish for the flowers
- Black polish or a contrasting polish for the flowers
- A thin nail art brush
- Acetone or nail polish remover
- Top coat

Step by step

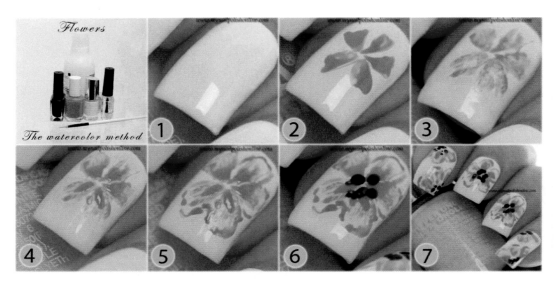

1. Start by applying the base coat then add one or two coats of top coat. The top coat acts as a shield for the base when you use the acetone/nail polish remover for the watercolor effect.
2. Paint flowers with the contrasting polish.
3. Using the watercolor technique, wash out the petals with acetone/nail polish remover as in the Watercolored technique described in Chapter "WaterColor".
4. Add a little bit of color in the center of the petals with the nail art brush.
5. The flowers can be left as in step four or you can add a contour to them depending on the effect you want to obtain. Compare the picture in step four and five before you decide which one you prefer.
6. Add some dots in the middle of the flowers using the second contrasting polish and the nail art brush.
7. Top coat the manicure.

Suggested color combinations

Watercolored flowers look great over white, off-white and creme colors. Depending on the base one can use pastels as backgrounds together with darker shades of the same color. Always try to choose a contrasting color for the flowers compared to the base. The washed-out effect is more visible with a contrasting color. Some color combinations that can be used are:

- White backgrounds can be combined with pink, red, blue, yellow and purple colors
- Creme backgrounds can be combined with red flowers as in the picture above
- Light blue or white backgrounds can be combined with dark blue or purple flowers as in the left picture below
- Pink backgrounds can be combined with dark pink/magenta or purple flowers

Advanced techniques

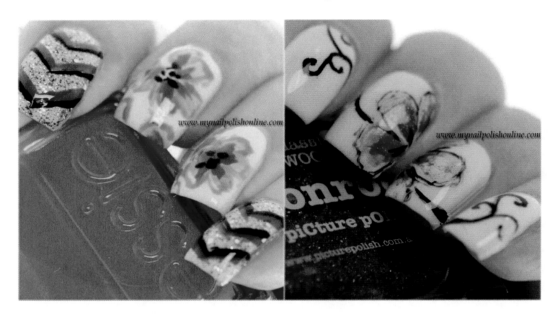

The watercolored flowers can be combined with many other techniques and patterns like chevrons and dots. In the left picture above they are done as accent nails and in combination with chevrons. The flowers can be done very small or very big as in the right picture above where they go over two nails forming a flower when the nails are put together.

CAMOUFLAGE NAILS

The camouflage nails look intricate and are fun and easy to do. The classic colors are greens, browns, sand colored and black but there are other colors that are working just as great together in a camouflage nails design.

Materials/Supplies

This is what you'll need for painting camouflage nails:
- A polish for your background
- A couple of polishes for the camouflage spots
- A dotting tool
- Top coat

Step by step

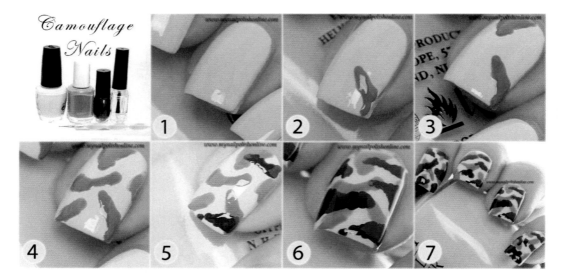

1. Start by applying the base polish.
2. Take one of the polishes that were meant to be used for the spots and start painting a spot using a dotting tool.
3. Applying a second spot with the same color. Apply the spots randomly and leave room for the other color.
4. Continue applying spots with the first color.
5. Apply random spots with the second color. Try to paint the colors on top of each other as well as next to each other.
6. You should be able to see some of the background color when you're finished with the application of the second color.
7. Clean up the cuticles with a nail art brush and nail polish remover or acetone. Top coat the manicure.

Suggested color combinations

When painting camouflage designs you should pick colors from the same color range, like:

- Different shades of green, brown, nude and black
- Different shades of pink and gray
- Different shades of blue as in the picture above
- Different shades of gray and yellow

Advanced techniques

The technique can be combined with half moons where the half moons are painted on top of the camouflage nails. You could also combine camouflage nails with French tips on top of the camouflage pattern. Experiment with different combinations and find your favorite.

CHEVRONS

There are different kinds of chevrons but most of them can be painted either by freehanding or by using guides. The freehanding technique is hard to realize flawless but it's much quicker than the technique using guides.

Freehanding Chevrons

This might be one of the easiest yet most difficult way to paint chevrons depending on your freehanding skills. This technique might not be your favorite if you are a perfectionist because regardless of how steady you are on your freehanding, it's still hard to paint those absolutely perfect chevrons. With a little practice you can go a very long way though.

Materials/Supplies

This is what you will need to freehand chevrons:

- A polish for your background
- A small nail art brush
- Polishes for your chevrons
- Top coat

Step by step

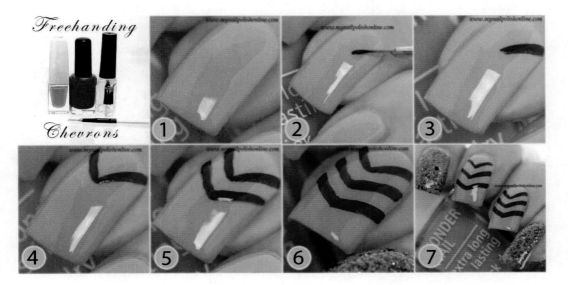

1. Apply the base polish of your choice and top coat it with a fast drying top coat.
2. Start painting chevrons from the middle of the nail.
3. Continue the line to the cuticle.
4. Paint a similar line on the other side of the nail forming a "V"-letter.
5. Paint a second chevron under the first one.
6. Paint as many chevrons as you wish under the two chevrons. You can always correct a line by making it thicker or by removing the unwanted lines with a nail art brush and some nail polish remover. Remember to be quick with the removing part and to not persist too much on the same spot or your base polish will dissolve and you will end up with a bald spot.
7. Clean up the cuticles and top coat the manicure.

Using guides for chevron

www.mynailpolishonline.com

The chevrons done by using guides should come out pretty perfect. There are guides to buy from different places and if you don't find ones that you like you could do your own by buying a pair of chevron cutting scissors and a piece of tape that you cut and place on your nails.

Materials/Supplies

The materials needed for freehanding chevrons are:
- A polish for your background
- Chevron guides
- Polishes for your chevrons
- Top coat

Step by step

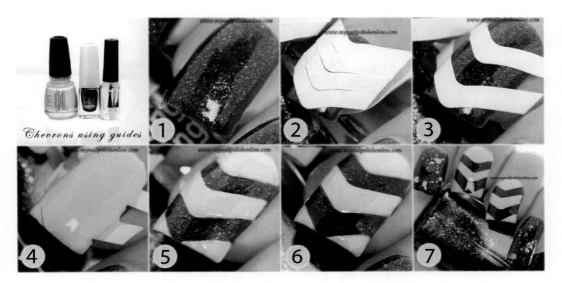

1. Apply your base color and let it dry completely. Use one coat of fast drying top coat to speed up the drying process. The polish should be absolutely dry before you precede with the next step.
2. Apply the guides on your nails.
3. Remove some guides in between.
4. Apply the polish chosen for your chevrons over the whole nail including the guides.
5. Wait for the polish to dry a little bit then remove the guides. The polish applied for the chevrons shouldn't be completely dry or you'll have problems removing the guides.
6. Cleanup your cuticles if necessary.
7. Top coat the manicure.

Suggested color combinations

Try contrasting colors for the chevrons:
- Use light backgrounds with dark chevrons
- Neon bases work well with dark chevrons
- Yellow works great with purple
- Red, green and white would look great for a Christmas chevron manicure
- Black or navy backgrounds look great combined together with gold

You could also go with subtle looks like:
- White and silver
- White and gold
- Different kinds of pink, purple, green etc.

Advanced techniques

Use chevrons together with other types of graphical techniques as stripes and dots. You could also use chevrons on a couple of nails and glitter or flowers on the other nails. A great combination would also be using glitter under the chevrons as in the picture above.

IKAT

IKATs are a lot of fun wearing and look intricate without being too difficult to paint. The irregularities of the shapes make this pattern fun and authentic. The IKAT are supposed to look like woven fabrics and the lines are symbolizing the thread that goes from one color to another. There are some patterns that are usually done in nail art and the first of them is the one that is most used.

Rhombus IKAT

The first pattern looks like rhombus on your nails. It can be varied by painting one big rhombus in the middle or several smaller placed here and there on the nail.

Materials/Supplies

For obtaining the pattern above you will need:
- A nail polish for the base
- A colored polish for the IKATs preferably in a contrasting color to the base color
- A white and a black polish
- A thin/striping nail art brush
- Top coat

Step by step

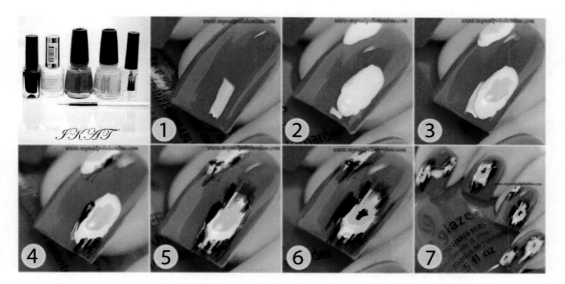

1. Paint your nails in the chosen base color and let the base dry completely. It helps adding a fast drying top coat to speed up the drying process.
2. Start by doing irregular shapes on the nails directly with the brush coming from the white polish or with a dotting tool.
3. Inside the white shapes paint some smaller irregular shapes with the color of your choice. These shapes look a lot like the white shapes but they are much smaller.
4. Start painting small black lines with the striping nail art brush going half way over the base and half way over the white shape.
5. Continue painting small black lines around all the white shapes. You want these lines to be thin and distinct.
6. With the same technique as the above start doing black areas inside the colored shape.
7. Seal the result with one coat of fast dying top coat.

Chevron IKAT

For this type of IKAT you need to work with small and thin vertical lines. The lines will cover each other so they don't need to be perfect. Try painting small thin lines on a piece of paper first for practicing.

Materials/Supplies

This is what you need for Chevron IKATS:
- Nail polish for the base
- A couple of polishes for the IKAT
- A black polish
- A thin/striping nail art brush
- Top coat

Step by step

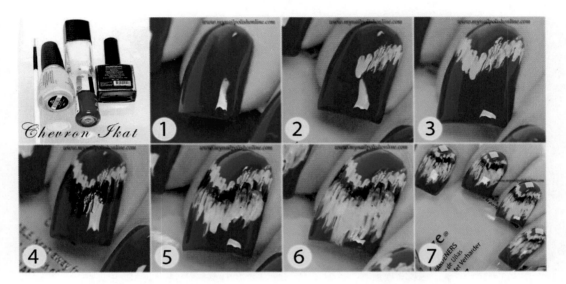

1. Paint your nails in the chosen base color and let it dry completely. It helps adding a fast drying top coat to speed up the drying process.
2. Start by painting small lines going from the middle of your nail to one side stopping at the cuticle.
3. Continue painting small vertical lines to the other side of the nail in form of a V.
4. Using the same technique as above paint small and thin vertical lines with the second color overlapping the first lines.
5. Continue the same way with the next color.
6. Repeat this with all the colors you want to use in your IKAT.
7. If you wish, add a stud on each nail, next to the cuticle. Apply one coat of fast drying top coat to seal the design.

Suggested color combinations

The black and the white should always be used because they add contrast to the IKAT-pattern and we want to make the new colors pop. Besides them try combining:
- Green and blue
- Blue and yellow
- Pink and purple

Advanced techniques

Try adding one or two more colors. In that case the design should be bigger for the different colors to be visible enough.

SARAN WRAP

Saran Wrap is a great basic technique that looks fantastic in itself and as a background to other nail arts. Depending on the chosen colors it can stand out or be subtle and classy, the difference is the color combination. The saran wraps work great with creme polishes but the combination of creme and shimmer can look beautiful too.

Materials/Supplies

The materials needed for the Saran Wrap technique are:
- Nail polish for the base
- Nail polish for the saran wrap
- A piece of plastic for the saran wrap
- A piece of paper to practice on
- Top coat

Step by step

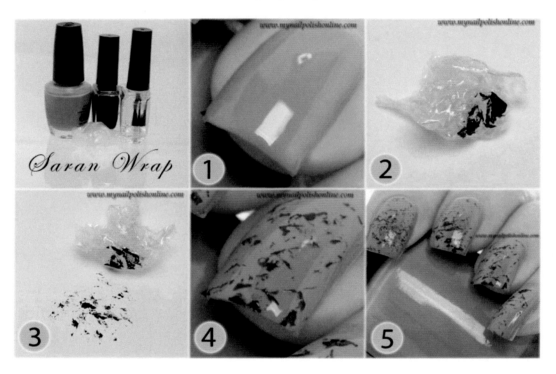

1. Paint your nails in the chosen base color and let it dry completely. It helps adding a fast drying top coat to speed up the drying time.
2. Take a piece of plastic that you crinkle and paint some nail polish on it.
3. Take a piece of paper and try sponging the pattern on the paper first.
4. Once you're happy with the result on the paper, continue on the nails.
5. Seal the result with one coat of fast dying top coat.

Suggested color combinations

For subtle nail arts or backgrounds, try using colors that are close color-wise, like different shades of pink or blue. For contrasting backgrounds, try using contrasting colors like black and white. Depending on the amount of the sponged polish you can create more or less subtle backgrounds. Some color combinations that can be used with this technique are:

- White/off-white and gray/black as in the right picture above
- Yellow and gray/black
- Neons and contrasting colors as gray/black
- Different shades of the same color like like dark blue and light blue

Advanced techniques

The saran wrap technique is a great base for other nail arts. Continue by freehanding flowers, butterflies or whatever comes to your mind on top of your saran wraps like in the right picture above.

FEATHERS

Feathers can look so delicate on the nails! Wear them as accent nails or on every nail, either way they will give your manicure that extra something. To master the feathers practice painting them on a piece of paper first and when you are happy with the result paint them on your nails.

Materials/Supplies

This is what you need for the feather nail art:

- A polish for your background
- One or two polishes for the feathers
- A small nail art brush
- Top coat

Step by step

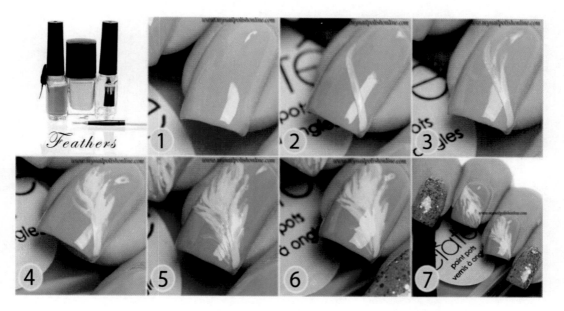

1. Start by applying the base polish of your choice.
2. Paint a stroke that will be the middle part of your feather.
3. Continue with small brush strokes to build up the feathers on one side of the middle stroke.
4. Paint in a similar way strokes on the other side of the middle stroke.
5. Paint strokes on both sides until you are finished. You could also ad a second color here and there or at the top of your feathers. This part is optionally but it will emphasize the feather a little bit.
6. Clean up if necessary.
7. Top coat the design.

Suggested color combinations

You could either go with light colored backgrounds and darker feathers or dark colored backgrounds and light colored feathers. If you choose the lighter colors on dark backgrounds, you should use polishes that are opaque for the feathers otherwise they won't turn up the way you want them to on the darker background. Some colors that look great together are:

- White/off-white backgrounds and black/gray/pink/teal feathers as in the picture above
- Pink backgrounds and purple feathers
- Lavender backgrounds and black feathers
- Navy blue backgrounds and silver/white/gold feathers
- Dark forest green backgrounds and gold/white feathers

Advanced techniques

Applying a touch of glitter here and there is a cool effect for your feathers. You could also paint the feathers on top of a saran wrap background, a watercolor background as in the picture above or maybe a gradient in appropriate colors.

HALF MOONS

To get a great looking half moon manicure is actually easier to do that one might think. Depending on your patience or steady hand you can achieve a half moon manicure in two ways, by using guides or by freehanding it.

Using guides

This method is preferred if you aren't steady on your hand but it requires you to have patience to leave the base polish to dry entirely before you continue with the half moons.

Materials/Supplies

The following materials are needed for painting half moons using guides:
- Nail polish for the base
- Guides for french manicures. You could also use tape if you like.
- Nail polish for the half moon
- Top coat

Step by step

1. Paint your nails with the chosen base color and let it dry completely. It helps adding a fast drying top coat to speed up the drying process. The base polish needs to be entirely dry before proceeding with the next step or your guides will stick to the base and the base will follow with the guides leaving bald spots.
2. Place the guides or your tape at near the cuticles leaving a half moon.
3. Paint the half moon with the second polish.
4. Wait for a little while (not too long though, the added polish shouldn't have dried completely) and remove the guides.
5. Seal the result with a coat of fast drying top coat.

Freehanding

This is the method for you if you have a steady hand or if you (like me) don't have the patience to wait for the base polish to dry before proceeding with the next step, the painting of the half moons.

Materials/Supplies

The materials needed for this technique are:
- Nail polish for the base
- A thin nail art brush
- A polish for the half moons
- Top coat

Step by step

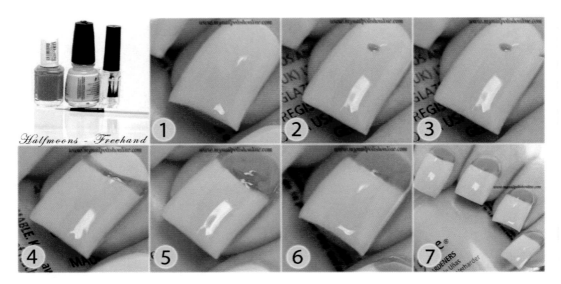

1. Start by painting the nails with the color of your choice. Let the base color dry a little bit (this means that you can touch the surface without leaving any marks on the surface). You could also wait for the polish to dry completely if you want. Use a fast drying top coat to speed up the process.
2. Place a small dot in the lowest part of the half moon with the nail art brush dipped into the polish used for the half moon.
3. Place a second dot at your cuticle as a guide for the half moon.
4. Place a dot at the cuticle on the other side of the nail and connect the three dots with a line creating a half circle.
5. Paint the rest of the half moon with the nail art brush.
6. Clean up the cuticles.
7. Seal the half moons with one coat of fast drying top coat.

Suggested color combinations

The possibilities of combining half moons are endless. You could combine almost any colors and they will work. Try using different kinds of finishes too, like creme with shimmers or glitter with cremes. If you want to go for subtle half moons you could use:

- Light blue and soft pink
- Soft pink and gold
- White and gray

For a more dramatic look you could use:

- Red and gold
- Black and gold/silver
- Navy blue and white/gold/silver
- A pastel (mint, pink etc.) and black/gold as in the right picture above

Advanced techniques

One easy way to give this manicure the extra something is to paint a small line just below the half moon, just between the half moon and the base. You could also do different patterns on the lower part of the nail, like dots, flowers or leopard spots.

STRIPES

It takes a steady hand to freehand stripes but that could be a solution if you don't have the patience to wait for the base polish to dry completely or if you don't have the patience to place the stripes on the nails. However, stripes look cool both as backgrounds and on their own. The color combination of the stripes will give them the feeling you want them to have, subtle or eye catching.

Freehanding stripes

A steady hand is required for freehanded stripes. Exercise on paper before you start practicing this technique on the nails.

Materials/Supplies

The materials needed for freehanded stripes are:
- A polish for your background
- One or several polishes for the stripes
- A small nail art brush
- Top coat

Step by step

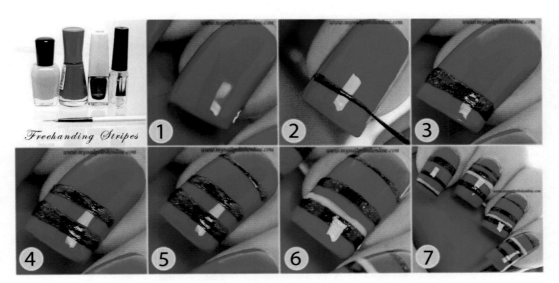

1. Start by applying the base polish of your manicure.
2. With the small nail art brush, start painting a stripe from one side of your nail to the other. Try rotating the nail instead of the brush to gain more control over the line.
3. Keep the thickness of the line or reinforce it until you are happy with the thickness of the stripe.
4. Paint a second stripe with the same technique as above.
5. Paint as many stripes you like to have on the nails.
6. If you wish you could paint a different colored stripe or two next to another stripe.
7. Clean up the cuticles and top coat the manicure.

Using tape

This technique will require that the base color of your manicure is completely dry. Taped stripes are very precise looking and well worth the time waiting for the base polish to dry.

Materials/Supplies

This is what you need for the taped stripes:
- A polish for your background
- One or several polishes for the stripes
- Tape
- Top coat

Step by step

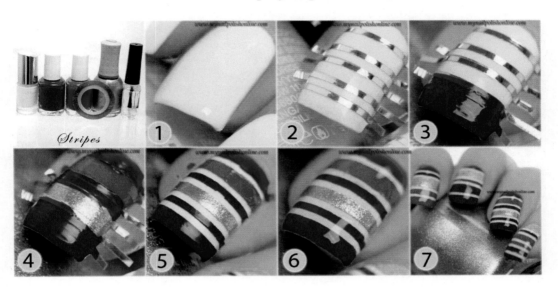

1. Start by applying the base polish of your manicure and let the base polish dry completely. A fast drying top coat will help the drying up process.
2. Add tape in an ordered way or just random.
3. Start by applying the other polish/polishes between the tapes. The tapes will be removed afterward so you won't have to worry about covering the tapes.
4. Continue with the other colors if you use more than one color.
5. When the newly applied polish is half dry, remove the tapes. Don't wait for the top polish to dry completely before you remove the tape but be sure to not remove the tapes too early either. The polish should have started to dry though.
6. Remove the excess polish from the cuticles.
7. Top coat the manicure.

Suggested color combinations

Dark and light colors make great eye-catching stripes, but so do neons and whites. For subtle manicures use a nude base and silver/white polishes for the stripes as in the right picture below. Some colors that look great together are:

- White, navy blue and red
- Nude white and silver
- Burgundy creme, gold and silver
- Pale blue, lavender or light pink with white stripes

Advanced techniques

Use stripes together with roses for a vintage feeling. Place stripes in different directions to form geometric shapes as in the left picture above.

GALAXY NAILS

To build up a galaxy on your nails you need a little bit of patience and a lot of polishes. Start by studying galaxy pictures first to get an indication of the colors you want to use. Each galaxy should be a little different even if the color range should stay the same from one nail to the other.

Materials/Supplies

This technique is material heavy. This is what you will need for painting Galaxy Nails:

- A dark polish for your background
- A white polish for the galaxy and stars
- Some colored polishes
- A small part of a sponge. Cut a bit of your kitchen sponge or of a make up sponge.
- A pair of tweezers
- A piece of paper
- A small dotting tool or a toothpick
- A nail art brush
- Top coat

Step by step

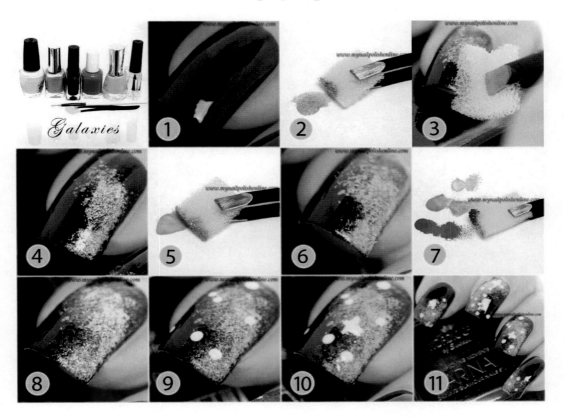

1.   Apply the dark polish that you wish to have as a base of your manicure.
2.   Put a little bit of the silver polish on the piece of paper. Take the sponge with the tweezers and dip it into the silver polish and sponge the excess polish on the paper.
3.   Start to build the galaxy by sponging the silver colored polish on the nail.
4.   You'll have to leave some dark space unsponged for the next colors and for the dark background.
5.   Take the next color and put a little bit of it on the paper. With the same sponge repeat sponging the polish on the paper to remove the excess polish.
6.   Apply the next color next to the silver color overlapping it here and there.
7.   Repeat step two with the next polish.
8.   Sponge the next color onto the nails with the same technique as above in step six.
9.   When you're happy with the galaxies, add stars with the dotting tool/toothpick.
10. Paint some cross formed stars here and there with a small nail art brush.
11. Clean up the cuticles if necessary with a nail art brush and a little bit of nail polish remover or acetone. Top coat your galaxies.

Suggested color combinations

The traditional way of doing galaxies are on dark backgrounds. Use a black/navy/dark purple polish as a background and do red based, blue based or yellow based galaxies. White is always a great color for the stars but you could also use silver or yellow instead of white.

The background could be a creme but it could also be a shimmer or a holographic polish. The same goes for the rest of the colors. Choose at least one shimmer, it will give the galaxy an extra glow.

Advanced techniques

Galaxies are quite advanced and complex by themselves and look best on their own. If they are a little bit too much you could use them as accent nails.

SPLATTERS

Before you start doing splatters, you've got to know that they are messy! Nevertheless the end result is so fascinating in it's randomness that they are definitely worth trying!

Materials/Supplies

The following materials are needed for doing splatters:
- A polish for your base
- A couple or three polishes for the splatters
- A big paper to protect the surroundings
- A straw
- Tape
- Top coat

Step by step

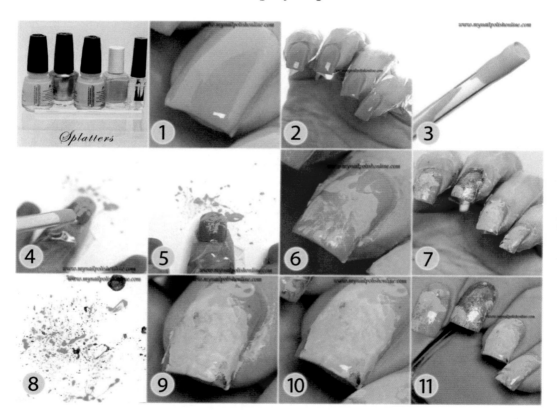

1. Apply your base coat and let it dry.
2. Tape around the nails to protect the fingers from the excess polish that will land on your fingers while creating the splatters.
3. Dip a straw into one of the colors. Be sure to dip it just a little bit just to get some polish at the end of the straw, otherwise you will end up with too much polish on the nails.
4. Place your fingers over a big piece of paper that will protect the surroundings from the splatters. Aim the straw at your nails by holding it at about three cm (about one inch) from your nails. Blow through the straw and watch the splatters land on your nails.

5. The splatters will land partially on your nails and on the protecting paper. They might also land on your protected cuticles.
6. Repeat until you are happy with the first color.
7. Repeat the process in steps 3-6 above with the rest of the colors until you are happy with the amount of splatters/polish that have landed on your nails.
8. After you're done the work space could look like this.
9. Remove the tape that is protecting your cuticles.
10. Clean up around the cuticles.
11. Top coat the manicure.

Suggested color combinations

Most colors work together in splats even if some work better than others. Here are some suggestions:

- A white base with yellow/green/black splats as in the left picture above
- A pastel base with a darker shade of the same color and a metallic. E.g. you can choose a light pink and a medium pink with a metallic purple as splatters or a baby blue base and a navy blue with a metallic blue for the splatters.
- A navy blue base and a light pink with a gold for the splatters

Advanced techniques

A great way of combining splatters is by doing just one splatter nail as an accent as in the left picture above and combine the used colors in other nail arts, like gradients or dotticures. You can also frame the splatter nail with the base color or a contrasting color. Because the splatter nails are crowded by themselves, make sure to do simpler designs on the other nails to let the splatters stand out from the rest of the nails.

NEEDLE MARBLING

The water marbling can be a little bit frustrating if something goes wrong and there are at least a couple of parameters that can go wrong as we've seen in the Water Marbling Chapter. The needle (or nail art brush) marbling gives a result that reminds of water marbling and it's a little easier to obtain than water marbling.

Materials/Supplies

The materials needed for needle marbling are:
- Nail polish for the base
- One or two polishes for the marbling
- A needle, a small dotting tool or a small nail art brush
- Top coat

Step by step

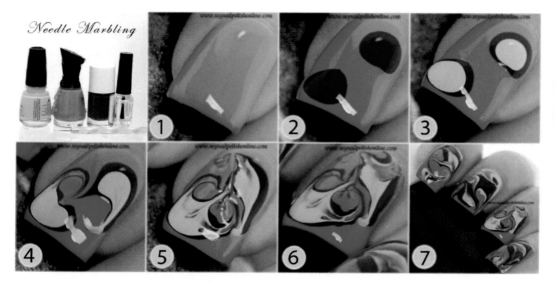

1. Start by painting your nails with the base color of your choice. You shouldn't top coat this because we want the polish to be sticky for the nail art.
2. Apply one or two drops of color with one of the polishes.
3. Apply one or two drops of color with the second polish. You might want to place the second drop on top of the first drop. This step is only required if you use two extra polishes for the needle marbling.
4. Take a needle, a dotting tool or a small nail art brush and draw patterns or swirls from the middle of the colored drops.
5. Continue by drawing patterns into the colors with the needle, the dotting tool or the small nail art brush.
6. Work both from inside of the color drops and from their outside.
7. When finished apply the top coat.

Suggested color combinations

White goes along with most of the other colors and so does black. You should choose opaque polishes thought because it's easier to get great results with them. Consider using several shades of the same color too. These colors look great together:
- Pink and purple
- Blue and purple
- Green and blue
- Pink and gray
- Gray and yellow

Advanced techniques

Besides creating marbling looking manicures this technique look great in creating patterns like connected hearts and flowers as in the picture above described in chapter "Flowers using needle marbling". Use the needle marbling as accent or on all nails.

WATER SPOTTED

The water spotted technique is much easier to achieve than the water marbling technique and you can get such great results using it!

Materials/Supplies

The materials needed for the water spotted technique are:
- A polish for your base
- A polish for the spots
- A cup with water
- Tape
- Hair spray
- Q-tips
- Top coat

Step by step

1. Apply the base polish and let it dry. To speed up the process, apply a fast drying top coat.
2. Tape around your nails.
3. Take a plastic cup and fill it with room temperated water. Take the polish of your choice and drop some drops into the water. The polish should be spread on the water surface. If the drops are sinking to the bottom, you'll need to repeat the process and take less polish with the brush.
4. You'll have to act fast now because the polish dries fast on the surface of the water and we need the polish to still be wet and formable. Take the hair spray

and spray close to the surface. There should form some patterns now on the surface. If you don't achieve the expected result, remove the pattern with a Q-tip and try again. Experiment with holding the hair spray at different distances from the water surface if you don't get the desired result.

5. Slowly dip one (or several) of your nails into the pattern.
6. While having the nail/nails into the water, take the Q-tip and catch the excess polish from the surface of the water.
7. Slowly take your nail/nails out from the water.
8. The excess polish has now fastened on the tape.
9. Remove the tape from the dipped fingers.
10. Clean up the excess polish. Let the water from your dipped nails dry or carefully remove the excess water with some tissues.
11. Apply a top coat for extra protection of your design.

Suggested color combinations

There are so many combinations that would look amazing with this technique! Here are some suggestions though:
- A minty base with black spots
- A green base with black or white spots
- A neon base with black spots as in the left picture above
- A pink base with gold spots

Advanced techniques

The technique works very nicely to double dip! To double dip means that after dipping your nails into the first color, you repeat the process with a second color. Try using e.g. a green base that you double dip into a white and a black pattern as in the right picture above. You could finish the design by adding funky French tips or half moons with the same color as your base or with the same color as the water spots. You could also add some studs or rhinestones at the end if you like.

DREAMCATCHERS

Dreamcatchers may look complicated at start but they are actually easy to do and they begin with a half circle at the cuticle of your nails. Dreamcatchers may come in many different shapes and designs but all of them involve freehanding. The great part about this is that the freehanding part is not so complicated as one might think.

Materials/Supplies

The following materials are needed for the Dreamcatchers:
- A polish for your background
- A couple of polishes for the dreamcatchers
- A small nail art brush
- A dotting tool or a toothpick
- Top coat

Step by step

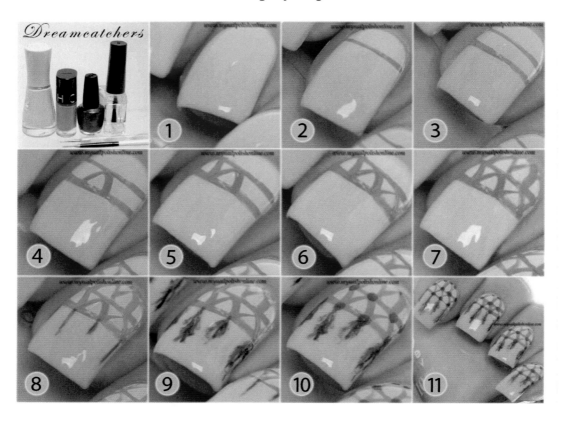

1. Start by applying the base polish of your manicure.
2. Paint a straight line close to your cuticle with a contrasting polish. You could also paint the line as a half circle if you want.
3. Paint a smaller second line between the first line and the cuticle.
4. Connect the two lines by painting small lines that go from one line to the other.
5. Continue painting small triangles between the two lines going out to one side of the nail.
6. Continue now from the center to the other side of the nail.
7. Paint small triangles from the upper line to the cuticle.
8. Take the second contrasting color and paint small lines going from the points where the lines are meeting on the first line you've painted in step two.
9. Paint small feathers at the end of the hanging lines. The tassels are painted the same way as feathers are painted in Chapter "Feathers".
10. With the dotting tool place dots at the connections between the lines and between the lines and the feathers.
11. Cleanup around the cuticles and top coat the manicure.

Suggested color combinations

Dreamcatchers look great with pale backgrounds and brown or black dreamcatchers. There are several ways to go though:

- Light background as pale pink, light green or minty blue with brown dreamcatchers and pink/orange dots
- Pale pinks with neon pinks or dark magenta for the dreamcatchers and black for the dots
- A neon green with dark brown or black dreamcatchers and white dots
- Pale pink as background, orange dreamcatchers and green feathers and dots as in the picture above

Advanced techniques

Dreamcatchers will look great over saran wraps, watercolored backgrounds and gradients. They work nicely on their own or as accent nails. You can also add bigger feathers on some of the nails keeping dreamcatchers on the other nails as in the picture shown in the sub chapter "Suggested Color Combinations" above.

WATER MARBLING

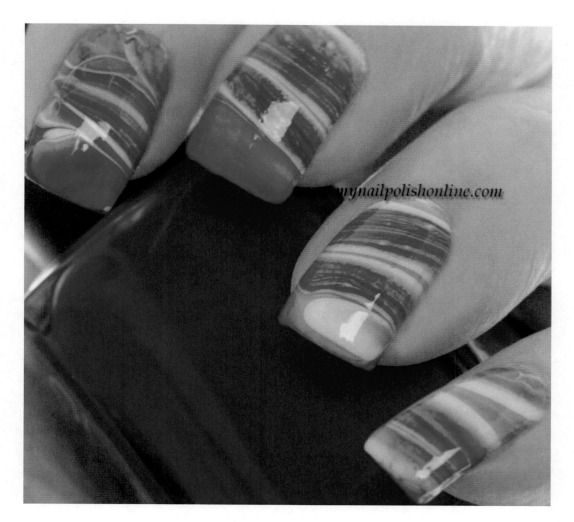

Water marble is a classic technique when it comes to nail art. The patterns, the designs and color combinations are endless but they are all based on the same technique, the same way of mastering the polish floating on the surface of the water. The best way of learning this technique is by experimenting until you've nailed it.

The technique is messy and it could be frustrating but if you manage to get the results you want it could be incredibly rewarding. The choice of polishes plays a big role in getting great results and if a combination of polishes doesn't work, switch to other polishes that might work better. Generally cremes work better than shimmers and neons but it's all a matter of experimenting the right polish pair. The water temperature is important too. Try using room temperated water.

Materials/Supplies

Water marble involves a lot of materials:
- A nail polish for the base
- A couple of polishes for the water marbling
- A cup of water
- A Q-tip
- Tape
- An orange stick, a toothpick or a dotting tool
- Top coat

Step by step

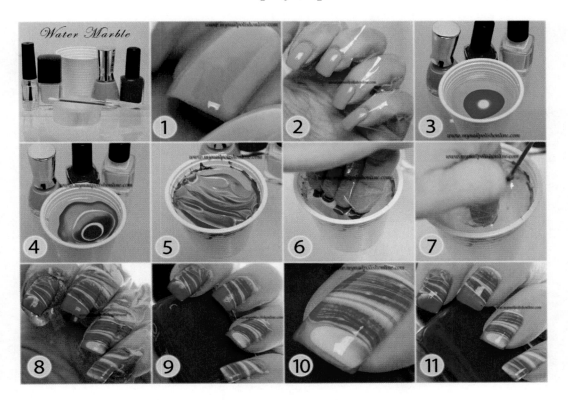

1. Apply your base polish and let it dry a little bit.
2. Protect your fingers and cuticles by taping around the nails.
3. Take a cup of water and start dropping one of the polishes on the surface of the water. The polish should start to spread evenly on the surface. If the polish sinks to the bottom you'll have to drop a smaller quantity of polish. If the polish doesn't spread try to steer along the sides of the cup with either the Q-tip or the orange pin. You have to work pretty fast. The polish that floats onto the surface dries fast. Drop the next drop of polish in the middle of the first drop. This polish should start spreading as well. If not, repeat the Q-tip or orange pin procedure described above. Do the same thing with the last polish.
4. Alternate the polishes three or four times the same way as in step three.
5. With the orange pin make some patterns into the polish circles. There are many shapes that can be made: zigzag, flowers, hearts and others.
6. Dip one or several fingers into the pattern.
7. Remove the excess polish with a Q-tip.
8. Remove the finger/fingers from the water. The pattern should now show on the nails and on the taped parts of the fingers.
9. Remove the tape.
10. Cleanup with a nail art brush and polish remover the excess polish from the cuticles.
11. Add a top coat.

Suggested color combinations

When you water marble search for polishes that contrast to each other colorwise. Try combining these colors:

- White with any other colors like blue, mint, pink or green
- Black with light pastel colors like light blue, mint or lilac
- Different shades of green as in the right picture above, pink or blue

Advanced techniques

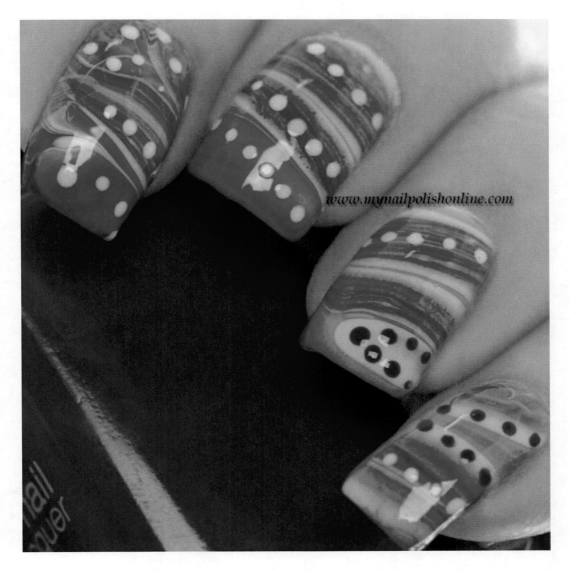

Some patterns work very nicely with dots. If you think the water marble is too much to wear on every nail it could be worn as an accent nail.

STAINED GLASS

This is such a cool looking technique when finished! The only down side of it is that is time consuming but it's oh so worth it!

Materials/Supplies

This is what you need for the Stained Glass technique:

- A polish for your background
- A small nail art brush
- A couple of polishes for the different pieces of glass
- A black polish for the lines
- Top coat

Step by step

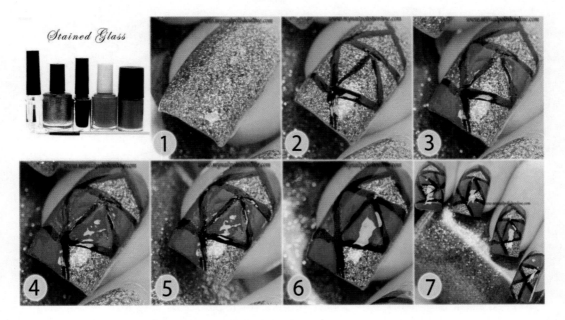

1. Start by applying the base polish.
2. With the small nail art brush and black polish paint some geometric shapes like triangles on your nails.
3. Fill in some of the spaces in between the black lines with the first polish. Leave room for the second color and for the background color to show.
4. Fill in some of the spaces left unfilled in step three with the second polish and alternate the colors randomly. Make sure some of the spaces are left unfilled for the base polish to show through.
5. Go over the black lines again with black polish. This will assure you that the black lines are still intact.
6. Clean up the cuticles.
7. Top coat the manicure.

Suggested color combinations

Think about the colors used in real stained glasses and try to emulate it on the nails. Use blue, orange and red together or green, orange and blue. You could also use non-classic colors like purple, yellow and turquoise as in the left picture above. Try working with three colors, that will give you the best result.

Paint white lines instead of black to obtain ceramic-looking nails. They look great with blues and aqua colored polishes.

Advanced techniques

Stained glass nails work very nicely on their own but work very nicely as accents. You could also paint a flower in the middle of the nails by using this technique, and fill in the rest of the nails with geometric forms.

FINAL THOUGHTS

I hope you've enjoyed reading and exploring the book as much as I've done doing it and that you've found some helpful tips and tricks for different nail arts. Some final thoughts:

- Remember that nail art should be fun!
- Play around with colors trying unexpected combinations and see what you like. Sometimes the favorites are created when you are stepping outside of your comfort zone.
- Practice makes perfect. If the nail art isn't perfect from the start it will improve gradually every time you are painting your nails.

I would love to have a visit from you at my nail art and nail polish blog "My Nail Polish Online" or one of my social media sites:

- Facebook - https://www.facebook.com/mynailpolishonline/
- Instagram - https://www.instagram.com/mynailpolishonline/
- Pinterest - https://www.pinterest.se/mynailpolishonl/
- Twitter - https://twitter.com/MyNailPolishONL
- Google+ - https://plus.google.com/u/0/108954405499949479531

Please let me know if you've used the book as help or inspiration in any nail art technique by tagging me on one of the social medias above or by just writing me an email. I would love hearing from you. Contact information is found on my blog "My Nail Polish Online", http://www.mynailpolishonline.com/

Made in the USA
Las Vegas, NV
29 December 2024

15555628R00090